Purple Darkness and Other Poems
By Jennifer Jo Fay
Photography by Jennifer Jo Fay

Purple Darkness

In a purple night with
no stars in sight,
how can one make
a wish to catch a silent dream?
Cold, cold air stings
my face, oh how I wish
for something new.
Purple night, nocturnal owl
wise beyond years yet
not knowing why he
can't see beyond the moment.
Purple night, I stand
near the bench as I
ponder what my next move
shall be. I guess I'll just
hang in this balance of life
taking the gift that's been
given to me. It's mine,
nobody else's.

Roller Coaster Love

Love likes speeding along
simply zooming.
Shooting star that it is,
can one hold on?
Taking flight like this
roller coaster, one needs
to slow down. Can love
be like a turtle, taking time
to nurture the unique bond
two lovers have for each other?
Slow down love, I tell you
slow down. I can't seem
to think! I don't want
this roller coaster to break!
Propelling too fast, I've only
known you a day! Who
are you anyway? Could this
Be real love? Or maybe just lust.

Emily Dickinson Reincarnated

I sit in my apartment thinking
of life. I've so far not quite
lived half a life, yet I've
overcome so much. I've loved,
I've lost and regained my
strengths.
Yet, I haven't quite written as
much as Emily Dickinson
yet I know of love.
I'm by myself now, don't quite
need a man. Maybe one would
be nice to share in one's dreams.
Haven't found him yet, but I
do have my kids. I thank their
father every day for them.
I'm a homebody, love to sit and
write all day if I can.
Writing down words, wishes and
thoughts about love.
I've loved hard, fallen apart and
rejuvenated again. Oh, did perhaps
Emily Dickinson find herself
refreshed every day?
Simple lives, simple dreams
quiet person, yet knowledgeable
in so many ways.

Cousins

A childhood evening spent
in Nana's living room, I burst
into song singing You Light up my life.
Nana and Grampy listening
with pride, a memory of a
loving family brings a smile
to my face.
Waking up in their house,
a sleepover to treasure,
She served me cereal and
orange juice, with loving care.
Memories of my cousin and I
sneaking into her house,
Nana didn't know we were there.
while our sisters waltzed in
talking to Nana. We were
hiding on them, but decided
to surprise them, so into the kitchen
we burst. We wanted those
delicious sprinkle cookies too.

Chasing Infinity

Moments, those countless atoms
connecting together seem
like something to chase.
Just how do you run after infinity?
The impossible dream, seems
to always be out of one's grasp.
No boundaries is infinity,
possibilities endless like
that of a burning sun.
Finding that pot underneath
the rainbow one just never knows.
Where does the sky end?
Infinity never does, so all we can do
is to gather what we can
and try our best to chase
what is tangible as infinity
is sort of invisible yet a
moment in time is countless
so ponder a dream.

Neighbors

One morning in the calm light
of a mid fall day, I was knitting
a sock. Simply quietly keeping
my idle hands busy. Purple
was the color. The air was crisp.
My neighbor came out, chatting
with me. He asked me to look
in on his wife while he gathered
himself, groceries he needed.
I knocked on her door, got no answer.
Coming back from my errand,
there were abundance of
ambulances. I knew something
was wrong. My neighbor was
upset. I should have gone in,
But what would I have found
it would have been traumatic.
She died that day. They brought
her down, nothing on lying
on the stretcher. Blue lips,
so near death. It was hard
to see. Her husband was
stunned, felt bad he had left.
Nothing could have been done,
she had been in so much pain.
In and out of breath, her life
floated on. A spirit in the wind,
she remains by his side.

Layers

Layers of onions, peeling away
like flesh to reveal a psyche
one didn't seem to know was there.
Mysterious onion, who are you
really? You haven't quite
said it all, so I know there's
so much more you haven't
told me yet. Layers, like
icy snow sheets only to be
broken with my purple boot.
Yet, there is so much more
underneath the surface
and you're not an open book.
That's okay, as we're all
supposed to have our secrets
We are allowed to take
to our silent graves.
Layers of onions we all seem to be.
Hold onto your onion, peel away
as you please. Tuck your
layers away and keep to yourself.

Growing Up

Her inner will, she has her own mind.
Child with her thoughts,
she's determined to be
the teen she is, her choices
are hers. Challenging she is,
but I love her no less.
My baby is growing up,
beautiful young lady she is.
Wants to eat healthy, great way
to be. Has thoughts of her own,
and wants to learn how
to be a doctor or into coding.
She may change her mind,
but it's up to her. She's got
time to decide, the moment
at hand holds her oyster,
it's hers.
I have mine, we all have
our choices. I applaud her,
love her and will have trust
in her ideas. She is my daughter,
so wonderful. I don't have a
favorite.

Collection of Pictures

A thousand pictures, a trail
to the sky share a rainbow
that's mine.
Mother gave birth, I came
into this world a baby so small.
Grammy wrote to her pupils,
it's a girl, Jennifer Jo.
Baby toys, blocks, dolls and
more. A picture of me climbing
a dresser, captured in a moment.
All these pictures I've glimpsed
millions of times in my mind.
They rest in a floral box
to be treasured forever.
What if the world had no pictures,
what would we do? We've
got to have them as reminders
of what we once were.
Memories, these thousand pictures
like constellations in the sky.
Maps of our roads we have
travelled in time. Millions of forks,
some not taken yet it's our road
that's ours with these thousands
of pictures.

Phasing of the Moon

Full moon, waxing moon, waning moon
these phases go round the sun,
like fragile changes in the wind
and a new day has come.
Lingering in a fraction of a second,
how fate will be. This silence
is breathtaking, in the phases
of the moon.
My cat, Luna lies still in the
blue chair nearby. I sit here
typing with emotions springing forth.
I shall get inspiration and call my
children. Their voices will
light my way.
These phases of the moon,
will too soon pass away
To reveal a fresh slate
to begin again.
These phases of the moon,
so necessary in life.

Magnetic Words

Written words, inspired thoughts
seem to be distracted as I sit here
and play. I'm busy on Face book,
Instagram and Twitter.
Get me back on track,
to write down my desires.
Magnetic words, I should dig them
out now and perhaps find out
what I need to say next.
Written words, written words
where are you going?
I need to stare at this blank page
I've got. Need to get propelling,
fingers clicking on this keyboard.
I know my left brain is thinking,
sending messages to my fingers.
Paper words, in an Edward Cullen
case. I wrote them on fine paper,
all those little cut out words.
Similar to magnetic words, to inspire
me to create. I should find them all
now and search for the concoction
that needs to be typed.
Do it now.

Babies

Baby boy, baby boy
I held you in my womb.
You pushed and prodded
making me spill my coffee.
I went into labor,
thought I was dying.
Sean.
Baby boy, baby boy
you poked me too,
made me drop my knitting.
You came out different,
but a special needs loving boy.
Jake.
Baby girl, baby girl
you did summersaults inside.
You made me drop my pen,
came out a surprise.
Thought I'd have all boys.
Mollyanne.
Baby girl, baby girl
you started moving early.
Made me toss and turn.
my little artist came out
the most beautiful surprise ever.
Julia.

Moderation

Too much of a good thing
can be choking at times.
Sometimes we need to learn
to cut ourselves back.
That belt won't buckle,
will it? Oh no, so what will
you do? Treadmill time
or a walk four miles away.
Sarah Lee pound cake
went straight to the pot.
Yes, filled it up so I'm feeling
like an airbag bloated and
weighted.
Just like the creative mind
can have too many thoughts.
One must edit, edit
cut back the words.
Loving too much, can peel away
the senses. Need time to think,
sit back and sift out what
is the most important in life.
Moderation is great, makes one
happy with less as it's
not having millions of material things
that is important in life.
Sometimes a blank wall
means so much more.

Broken Pretzel

Shattered soul, painful heart,
why must you feel so fragile?
Wretched raven, twisted pretzel,
your heart drenched in water.
Bloody water, lifeless mind,
get yourself out of your funk.
Do it now. Crimson tides,
wounded hill, you lost your will
but you need to climb out of the well.
See that angel up there
looking down on you now?
She's telling to see when
you cannot seem to see.
You've been blind, I tell you
and you've got to open those
deep eyes like the ocean it is.
There's copper stairs filled with
such good luck you know.
You can do it, yes you can
so lift your weary shoes
and fix your torn heart.
There's a world that needs you.

Smooth Glass

Tell me now of a calm lake
so cool and inviting. I need
to soak it up, take in it's
tranquility.
A lone yellow flower grows
by the sand while I rest upon
this polka dot beach towel,
with a graphite pencil in my hand.
Drawn out Bella Swan,
my favorite character by far.
Her image crystal clear,
my talented hands inspired by.
I look to the lake thinking quietly now
how nature is pure, untainted,
so powerful in it's simplicity.
I know that there will soon
be a storm to create friction
and waves, but for now I take
this smooth glass of watery mass.
For it's what I've got for the moment,
tomorrow's not promised.
To live in the present is all
one can really do.

Mine

Bitterness, criticism and petty words
sometimes seem to dig into this
thick skin like a serrated knife.
Book reviews, some nice and others
hurtful. Didn't like the description
of the purple dishcloth.
So what, it's purple.
I'm the author, the story is mine.
It's my choice, not yours.
I'll shrug it off, ignore,
be the mature writer I am.
You say a 12 year old wrote it?
I'm 48.
If you were to write it,
you'd be the author
and it wouldn't be mine.
So maybe my college student
in my novel should drink
Oval tine instead of gourmet coffee?
Maybe so. But she'll have
a white trash bin and she'll
dump it out tomorrow.
Yet, I'll take this criticism
with a grain of salt
and either decide to take
the advice and grow as a writer
or I will listen to my heart
and do what I want.
It's my story to tell.

Aging Scissors

Mother's scissors, aging black handles
used to rest in her case I looked at
as a young girl. Pretty basket,
with the satin floral pincushion top
underneath the cover, I remember
from long ago.
I thought I lost the scissors, perhaps
thrown them out in the dumpster
or given them away.
They didn't cut anymore, dulled
with passing time.
Memories of Mom, seated at her
Singer sewing machine,
making marble bags for
sister and I.
Not long ago, I found my scissors
and took some pictures of them
with silken flowers.
Now they rest in my handmade
Bella Swan jar with the hearts
and golden glitter.
Those scissors I cherish,
thoughts of Mother contained.
My beating heart shall think
of those scissors and know
I was loved.

A Walk Down the Block

Thought in dreams I'd walked a
thousand miles, well I ended
up walking a few blocks to
Jolley and came back with
a pasta salad and a soda.
Could you imagine walking
across country? What an
endurance. In essence,
we've all walked a thousand miles
down rough roads, cobblestones,
and the simple dirt ones as well.
A trillion different roads
there really seem to be.
A fork in the road and life's choices
bring us to decisions only we
must make. I was sitting in
my rust colored rocking chair
just deciding to venture out
or not. But, I sold some poetry books
and wanted a treat.
Not that soda is good of course,
but it's going to be a treat.
It shall keep me up so I can
keep writing on. Got dreams
to fill you know. Cold was
the moment as I braved
God's elements. I'm ready
to write and pour out my heart.
I may never get famous,
but I'll keep on trying as
you never know.

Flower Power Days

Living in the seventies,
growing up with bell bottom pants
I was a flower power child.
Shirley Temple, The Little Princess
and Saturday morning cartoons,
I sat with my siblings
while Mom visited with Nana
and friends in the kitchen.
We had no car seats, sat
in the way back or dangling
our feet from our uncle's pick up truck
was the best way to be.
Cousins and I all sitting,
singing 99 bottles of beer on the wall.
Had no Internet as outdoors
was our playroom.
Little House on the Prairie,
Laura Ingalls was my idol.
Once dreamed I was her friend.
Grew up on Mr. Rogers
and Sesame Street. Mr. Hooper
Was cool. Who can forget
Letterman? Or Zoom,
I had the record and remember it well.
Witches brew was my favorite song.
I still have my Princess Leia
barbie doll, but she's lost her donuts!
And Growing up Skipper's
boobs don't get bigger anymore.
I'm glad I grew up back then,
wouldn't wish it any other way.
However, I used to want to live
in the fifties or forties when my
Mom was growing up. I wanted
to know what it was like back then.
Seems like a long time ago,
but one can always travel back
and think about how things used to be.

Little Girl

Dark greenish ivy, with scattered veins,
trail up a red, brick wall of the old house
down the road.
Tilted lilac tree, holds on tight as nature
has spun it for a loop. Weathered the
ice storms and still stands strong,
like the child who holds a dream
in the palm of her hands.
She's been running home to her mother
with a bouquet in her hands.
Lilacs for Mom and fresh scents
to be shined upon.
Into the simple vase Mom pulls
from the hutch, go the flowers
for a decoration and love to foretell.
Little girl, an artist
draws pictures of Bun-bun, her
bunny rabbit toy she shall have all her life.
Ivy leaves, constant and fresh
life force to gather
as the girl ultimately grows up
just like her Mom.

Simplicity

What does a girl need?
Do you really need all that
material stuff that is collecting
dust upon your shelves?
Crystal goblets, trinket boxes
and all that yarn? I'm looking
at all my yarn and knowing
I shouldn't have gotten it all.
I've been writing now,
put the needles down.
But, I'll hold onto it as I
know I will knit again.
Weeding out can feel so good.
Living with less can be
so fulfilling.
I've given lots of things away,
to neighbors, to friends.
Clutter is gone, don't have
much left to weed.
But I've got my words and
my needles so that's all I need.
I've got the things that matter
the most. Simplicity sometimes
is the better way to be.

Raw

She didn't mean it. She said she
could hardly wait till I go. She
didn't mean it. I know in my heart
she loves me.
Just my teenage daughter,
frustrated with feelings.
The moment was raw,
she didn't mean it.
I love her so much.
Teenage daughter with her own will.
Said she was like her father.
I told her that's fine.
I love her just the way she is.
I know she loves me,
she's just in her element
being a teenager.

The Young Man

He once was a pin dot
in my belly. I could hardly
wait to be a new mother.
My baby came to be,
I watched him sleep and
felt the warmth of his baby cheeks
against my skin.
As he grew, he became
the social butterfly.
Friends flocked to our house,
they played video games,
traded cards and rode their scooters
all day long.
They started a fire with
a magnifying glass and leaves.
To my horror, it grew to fifteen feet.
As he grew, Dungeons and Dragons
was the thing. And visits from
friends as they laughed and pulled pranks.
He once taped a friend to a chair
with duct tape on his mouth. They
said he was being interrogated.
As my son grew, he graduated.
Such a proud moment for Mom and Dad.
He's now a young man going
to college on the other side of USA.
Studying archaeology and enjoying
new found freedom. Has a girlfriend,
who came to visit last summer.
I felt like chopped liver
when a girl was around.
He'll keep growing into a well
rounded man.
I love him so much and
he makes me so proud.
He once was my baby and
he will always be that,
but one day he'll grow into a father
someday and have kids of his own
to be proud of too.

The Unfinished Bench

I had a lovely unfinished bench once
in my early married years. For a while
it held some of my craft stuff, rested
at the end of our bed. The one with
the heart quilted comforter. The
comforter got holes, it's gone with
the past.
The bench later held presents for
Christmas and such, my children
secretly knew where the hiding place was.
It came to the new apartment with me,
after I divorced. It still held presents
and the old baby toys.
It came to another apartment with me
and still held the baby toys I cherished
so much.
It had baby books too, I was holding
them all.
Wanted to save them for grandchildren
but I'm not a Nana as of yet.
Finally, one evening I emptied it all
and put the bench out in the lobby
for the neighbors to have.
I got rid of most of the books
and the baby toys.
A neighbor wanted them for some
children in need.
I feel satisfied they went to a good home,
but made sure I kept my few favorite things.
I kept the wooden rattle, the Seadogs
baseball, a little green sweater I knitted
for Sean. Kept a few books like
Bunny My Honey.
I used to read it to my kids
and someday, I'll read it to grandkids
however, that's still a long time away.

Tea with Dad

Fireflies caught in a jar,
silken flowers upon her table
were a few things to love
forever in a time capsule.
Running in the darkness
watching fireflies in the air
simply flickering, mesmerizing.
I think I caught one once.
Nana's clothesline, towels hanging,
old worn clothespins in a fabric bag
still nestled in the kitchen closet
of my old childhood home.
Mom's china teacups dangling
on a shelf. The ones with green flowers
I remember. Sometime once again
when I visit my Dad, I shall drink
tea from one and treasure a moment
with my Dad. We'll talk about
the old days when Mom was alive,
share memories about her.
She was so much fun.
She was a happy drunk and
once wanted to climb onto
the doorknob. Silly old Mom.
I still miss her all the time,
but time heals a broken heart.

The Petunia

Somewhere in a garden of a
long forgotten day,
was a single purple petunia
with beads of raindrops upon
its petals. The brown earth
cradled it within a precious time
to call a quiet place of solitude.
The petunia lingered in the
days of sunshine, and in some
times of rain.
Upon a misty morning, it closed
up its petals only to reveal its
essence in the warmth of afternoon.
On moments in time, the gardener
came out to play. She'd plant her
flowers and pull some weeds
while sometimes falling backwards
as she pulled.
The petunia was there to inspire
and she went inside to think about
the beauty she had planted in
her lovely garden dreams.

Daisy Cat

Daisy cat, daisy cat
was a very pretty cat indeed.
She was a quiet cat
resting next to my lovely daughter.
A friend let them have the cat,
and they loved it.
She would quietly purr
and became the family cat.
My daughter loved her so,
and finally one day,
Christmas day to be exact,
she walked silently into
one of the bedrooms and
choked on her saliva.
My daughter felt incomplete,
they buried her in the backyard.
Daisy will always be remembered
as a cherished pet indeed.

Legacy

Self striping socks keep my feet warm,
while on a cold winter's day I think of
perhaps a mushroom pizza. Not sure.
Fingerless gloves, keep my hands warm
on another cold day as I take the bus
to visit the kids.
I'll hang out at the library before I see them,
a quiet place to write and nourish my thoughts.
Hens and chicks on my table, well watered
today seem to be growing a little.
Skating program in the background,
my white noise for today.
I've got to keep writing, keep going
I must.
I hope I don't get writer's block,
that has happened before.
That's when I pick up the needles
and knit some more socks, a headband
a hat.
Knitted one for my daughter,
lovingly done.
I guess that's just me, doing everything
with love. That's why I write,
I don't do it for fame,
don't do it for lots of money.
I do it for love.
I'm leaving a legacy
for my children, I do it for them.
But most of all, I do it for me.

Buddy

Here comes my friend and her
Pomeranian dog, Buddy.
He wags his tail and is excited today.
I open up my doors, and in they come.
What a sight to see,
It was funny, I tell you.
Ella cat, booked it into the bedroom
then she came back.
Luna cat arched her back and
so did the other.
Ella jumped up on the card table,
stayed there the duration.
Both hissed and meowed,
noises I'd never heard them
do before. It was a sight to see,
but won't happen again.
It didn't go over well, the cats and Buddy.
Luna and Buddy started a fight
among the skeins of yarn
and let's just say,
my cats don't like dogs!

9 781542 304474